Skateboarding Science

Helaine Becker

Crabtree Publishing Company

www.crabtreebooks.com

Crabtree Publishing Company

www.crabtreebooks.com

Author: Helaine Becker

Editors: Molly Aloian
Leon Gray

Proofreaders: Adrianna Morganelli, Katherine Berti
Crystal Sikkens

Project coordinator: Robert Walker

Production coordinator: Margaret Amy Salter

Prepress technician: Margaret Amy Salter

Designer: Lynne Lennon

Picture researcher: Sean Hannaway

Managing editor: Tim Cooke

Art director: Jeni Child

Design manager: David Poole

Editorial director: Lindsey Lowe

Children's publisher: Anne O'Daly

Photographs:
Action Images: Lucy Nicholson: pages 4–5, 8, 14–15; Mike Blake:
page 7 (bottom left)
Action Plus: Neil Tingle: page 6
Alamy: S. Kuttig: page 16; Joe Tree: pages 20–21; David Young-Wolff:
page 23 (top); Buzz Pictures: page 26
Buzz Pictures: Styley: page 12
ClimaxMfg: page 9 (top)
Corbis: Sam Diephuis: page 13 (top), 15; Roy Morsch: page 13 (bottom);
John-Francis Bourke: page 17; Martin Philbey: page 18; Sergey
Dolzhenko: page 19; Duomo: page 23 (bottom)
Gasoline Alley Antiques: page 11 (bottom)
Getty Images: Tony Duffy: page 5; Bill Ray: page 7 (top right);
Jeanne Rice: page 22; Tina Schmidt: page 24; Donald Miralle:
page 29 (bottom)
iStockphoto: Christian Carroll: backgrounds
Movie Store Collection: Amblin: page 28
OC Ramps Inc: page 25
PA Photos: Branimir Kvartuc: front cover; Gero Breloer: page 29 (top)
Rex Features: David Thorpe: page 7 (center right); Pekka Sakki:
page 10; Neale Haynes: page 27
Shutterstock: Alexander Kalina: page 9 (bottom)
Warren Bolster: Concrete Wave Editions: page 11 (top)

Illustrations:
Mark Walker: pages 11, 19

Every effort has been made to trace the owners of copyrighted material.

Library and Archives Canada Cataloguing in Publication

Becker, Helaine, 1961-
Skateboarding science / Helaine Becker.

(Sports science)
Includes index.
ISBN 978-0-7787-4536-5 (bound).--ISBN 978-0-7787-4553-2 (pbk.)

1. Skateboarding--Juvenile literature. 2. Sports sciences--Juvenile
literature. I. Title. II. Series: Sports science (St. Catharines, Ont.)

GV859.8.B42 2008   j796.2201'5   C2008-907434-3

Library of Congress Cataloging-in-Publication Data

Becker, Helaine.
Skateboarding science / Helaine Becker.
p. cm. -- (Sports science)
Includes index.
ISBN 978-0-7787-4553-2 (pbk. : alk. paper) -- ISBN 978-0-7787-4536-5
(reinforced library binding : alk. paper)
1. Skateboarding--Juvenile literature. 2. Sports sciences--Juvenile
literature. I. Title. II. Series.

GV859.8.B43 2009
796.22--dc22

2008048869

Crabtree Publishing Company

www.crabtreebooks.com   1-800-387-7650

Published in Canada
Crabtree Publishing
616 Welland Ave.
St. Catharines, Ontario
L2M 5V6

Published in the United States
Crabtree Publishing
PMB16A
350 Fifth Ave., Suite 3308
New York, NY 10118

Contents

Introducing Skateboarding

Imagine you're a Californian surfer. You like nothing better than to paddle out to the break and catch a wave. But what do you do when the ocean is as flat as a pancake? Wouldn't it be great if you could turn roadways into roadwaves for nonstop surf action?

That's exactly how the sport of skateboarding got its start. During the 1950s, restless surfers stuck wooden boxes onto rollerskate wheels. They rode their "skateboards" after the day's surfing was done. The new sport took off. By 1963, you could buy fancy skateboards across North America. The boards even came in customized designs for different riding styles, such as downhill or freestyle.

Skateboarding did not always enjoy such a smooth ride, though. The sport almost died several times. But it was reborn, again and again, each time in more exhilarating ways.

Skaters can do the most amazing acrobatic tricks on the vert ramp.

NEW WORDS

Grind: To ride on a ledge or rail in such a way that only the trucks touch, making a grinding noise.

4

LOOK CLOSER

Olympic sport

Not all skaters like the idea of skateboarding as an Olympic sport. They think it might force their sport to fit into an approved "mold." Many would like to keep the sport the way it is — independent and freewheeling. But if skateboarding were an Olympic sport, it would receive a lot more funding. Many more skaters might be able to turn the sport they love into a career.

Skateboard industry

Today, skateboarding is a multimillion-dollar industry. Top skaters are professionals who can make a career through prize money and sponsorship deals. Skateboarding might even become an Olympic sport. So get ready for a thrilling ride through the world of **half-pipes** and **half-cabs**, flips and turns, and slides and **grinds**.

Skateboarding has been a popular sport for many decades.

Half-cab: A ramp trick named for skater Steve Caballero.
Half-pipe: A U-shaped ramp used for skateboard tricks.

Standing Room Only

The first **decks** were made from wood. These soon gave way to plastics and other materials that made the boards easier to ride. Most skaters now prefer original decks made from the wood of the maple tree.

The invention of the **kicktail** in the 1970s was a major breakthrough to skateboard design. The kicktail helps skaters turn and flip the board with ease. Another big development was adding grip tape. Grip tape helps the feet "stick" to the deck.

The kicktail was added to the skateboard's basic design to make flips and turns much easier.

LOOK CLOSER

Making the board

1) Thin layers of maple are cut to shape.
2) Glue is applied to each layer.
3) The layers are stacked on top of each other.
4) The stack is placed in a mold.
5) The stack is pressed together while the glue dries.
6) Holes are drilled in the finished board to complete the deck.

NEW WORDS

Deck: The flat part of the skateboard on which the skater stands.

A gritty deck surface is helpful for doing tricks. So is a slippery underside. In the 1980s, a company called Santa Cruz released Everslick boards. They were made with a plastic undercoat. The coating lets the board slide across any surface.

Different decks

Skaters choose different decks for different riding styles. Vert skaters do tricks on ramps and other vertical or curved surfaces. They prefer wider decks. Street skaters mostly do tricks on flat ground. They like narrower decks that give a good "pop" — a lift off when the board is flexed. Longboards are mostly used for downhill racing or **cruising**. They can measure up to six feet (1.8 m) long and are shaped like surfboards.

Modern decks are made from environmentally friendly materials such as bamboo.

Stacking the decks

1950s–1960s
The earliest skateboards were made from shaped wood.

1970s Brightly colored banana boards made from flexible plastic became very popular. Ribs on the underside gave the deck support.

1970s Most boards were made out of thin layers of maple that were glued together. Some included high-tech materials such as aluminum or fiberglass.

1980s Decks became wider and longer for street skating. The upturned nose was added.

1990s-present
Skateboard manufacturers produce decks in many different materials and shapes. Most have found that springy, strong maple is the best material for a smooth ride.

Kicktail: The rise at the back of the deck.
Cruising: Using your board to move around.

Truck Technology

The trucks do much more than connect the wheels to the deck. Without trucks, the skateboard could not carve turns.

The trucks are the T-shaped metal housings that are found on the underside of the deck. The truck is made of three main parts: the baseplate, the hanger, and the kingpin bolt.

▲ *The trucks bolt onto the underside of the deck.*

LOOK CLOSER

Chicago pivot

The basic truck design is based on the "Chicago pivot." This type of truck was invented for rollerskate ballroom dancing in the 1920s. Specially designed trucks for skateboards were not available in stores until 1975.

Trucks apart

The baseplate is the flat part of the truck that bolts onto the deck. The hanger is attached to the baseplate. It holds the wheel **axles**. The hanger lies against a depression, called a pivot cup, in the baseplate. The pivot cup lets the hanger move in many directions. It works in a similar way as your shoulders, which let your arms move in many directions.

NEW WORDS

Axle: A rod that attaches to wheels and allows them to spin.
Bushing: A hollow sleeve used to reduce friction or motion in mechanical parts.

The last part of the truck is the kingpin bolt. It holds all the truck's parts together. Spongy pads around the kingpin, called **bushings**, cushion the pin when it moves. The softer the bushings, the easier it is to make the skateboard turn. The stiffer the bushings, the harder it is to carve that curve. You can change the bushings or adjust the kingpin nut for tighter turns or better control.

These trucks are made from aluminum, which is soft and weak but good for grinding.

LOOK CLOSER

Friction forces

When two objects rub against each other, there is always some **friction**. Friction slows things down and wastes energy. Bushings are important because they reduce friction between the skateboard's moving parts.

deck

baseplate

kingpin bolt

axle

hanger

Friction: The force that opposes the movement of two surfaces that are touching one another.

9

Wheels Revolution

The first skateboards had metal wheels, but they got rusty quickly and produced a bone-rattling ride. Next came clay wheels. They were much smoother, but they wore out quickly. They were also dangerous, because they did not grip the road well.

In 1971, a California surfer named Frank Nasworthy remembered seeing **urethane** wheels being made at a plastics factory owned by his friend's father. He thought the urethane wheels would work better for skateboarding than metal or clay wheels. So Nasworthy put together his first boards with urethane wheels.

Wheels come in a range of colors and styles.

LOOK CLOSER

How do bearings work?
Bearings reduce friction by putting smooth metal balls or rollers between two moving surfaces. The surfaces can then roll over the balls instead of sliding against each other.

NEW WORDS

Urethane: A hard-wearing plastic that can be molded into different shapes.

Frank Nasworthy set up Cadillac Wheels in 1971.

They were very fast but very easy to control. Nasworthy invested $700 — his earnings from a restaurant job — to start up Cadillac Wheels Company. By 1975, he was selling 300,000 sets of wheels a year.

Sealed wheels

Rough Rider bearings ushered in the next wheel revolution. Until 1975, the wheels used for skateboarding had ball bearings that dropped into the wheels. They were easily ruined by dirt from the road. Rough Rider's bearings were sealed inside the wheel. The innovation allowed the wheels to last longer and to go faster.

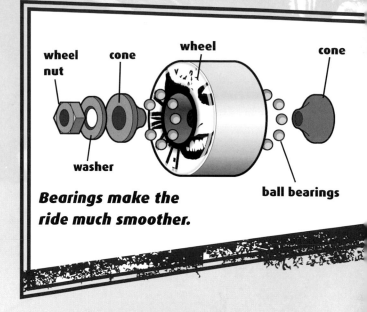

wheel nut cone wheel cone
washer ball bearings

Bearings make the ride much smoother.

RIDEMASTER LA. HABRA, CALIF.

LOOK CLOSER

What is urethane?

Urethane is a kind of hard, rubbery plastic. It is very **resilient**. When a resilient material is compressed or stretched, it returns to its original shape quickly. Urethane wheels keep in contact with the road better than wheels made from other materials. They lose less energy so they spin faster. They also absorb shocks better, making for a smoother ride.

Clay wheels were common until urethane took over in the 1970s.

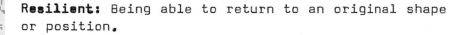

Resilient: Being able to return to an original shape or position.

Get a Grip

Most skateboarding shoes have vulcanized **soles, which help to grip to the deck.**

Skateboarding savvy only starts with your skateboard. What you wear on your feet is also key to clever skating. Your shoes can make the difference between a perfect pop shove-it and a pride-popping face-plant.

Skateboarding shoes need three elements. They should keep your feet on the deck with stellar grip. They should cushion you from jarring **impact**. And the shoes have got to be durable to survive pounding during tough sessions.

Skate shoemakers

In 1966, shoe manufacturer Vans released the first shoes that were dedicated for skateboarding. Other companies, such as Airwalk and Vision, followed suit with their own designs in the 1980s. New designs and materials keep making skate shoes better and better every year.

NEW WORDS

Impact: When two objects hit each other, such as your feet and the ground.

LOOK CLOSER

Shoe spotting

Look for skate shoes with these features:
1) Vulcanized rubber soles stick to the board and resist wear.
2) Air or gel pockets and thick cushioning prevent heel bruising.
3) Lace loops and shoelace protectors stop laces from shredding.
4) Flexibility in the sole increases board "feel."

⬆ *Skate shoes are not just a fashion statement. They aid grip and protect the feet from hard knocks.*

⬇ *Some skaters prefer to ride barefoot.*

FACT!

Foot facts

· The first skaters rode barefoot to honor the sport's surfing roots.
· Sneakers are considered to be safety wear to prevent foot injuries.
· If you ride with your right foot forward you are called a "goofy foot."

Vulcanized: Soles with sulfur added to the rubber to make it harder, stronger, and more stretchy.

Safe Skateboarding

Skateboarding is not all fun and games. Broken wrists and cracked heads are real risks for new and advanced skaters alike. Safety wear is crucial for reducing the crunch factor.

Early skaters did not have skate-specific safety gear. The best they could do was borrow the gear from other sports. It did not always work. Riders got injured. Skate parks were shut down. The sport was even banned in some places. The problem was solved when skate-specific helmets and pads with plastic caps came onto the market.

LOOK CLOSER

Basic first aid for broken bones

After calling for help from an adult or 911, follow these procedures:
1) Stop the bleeding. Apply pressure to the wound with a clean cloth.
2) **Immobilize** the injured area.
3) Apply ice packs. Ice reduces pain and swelling.
4) Treat for shock. Make the person lie down. Position their head lower than their body. Raise their legs slightly.

NEW WORDS

Immobilize: To prevent from moving.

Plastic protection

Knee pads and arm pads are made up of plastic caps that cover thick cushions. Since they reduce friction, the caps let you slide to safety if you fall. Wrist guards act like an **exoskeleton** to protect wrist joints. It is essential that new skaters wear the right gear. Even seasoned skaters should wear pads to protect against broken bones.

Helmet, arm pads, and kneepads — safety gear is vital to prevent injuries.

FACT! Safety first

Unlike most other sports, there are no performance standards for skateboarding safety gear. Choose your gear carefully!

LOOK CLOSER

Head protection

Helmets are designed to protect your head from hard knocks. An inner layer of foam absorbs energy and softens the blow to your brain. The best foam for board helmets is made from expanded polypropylene (EPP). A hard outer shell stands up to multiple impacts. A sturdy chin strap and buckle keep your helmet snugly in place. Keep it fastened at all times! A bright color makes you easier to see while street skating. An ASTM F1492 sticker means the helmet is the safest.

Exoskeleton: An outer skeleton or shell, like an insect.

Body Basics

Most skateboard professionals are serious athletes. They stay in shape and take care of their bodies to keep up with the demands of the sport. Take some tips from the top skaters before you tackle tricks of your own.

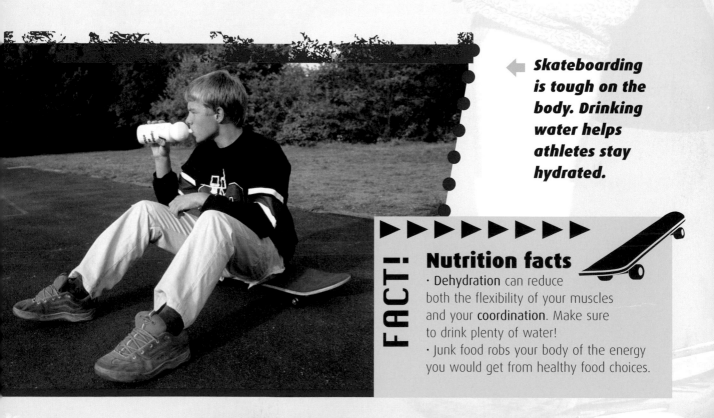

Skateboarding is tough on the body. Drinking water helps athletes stay hydrated.

FACT! Nutrition facts
· **Dehydration** can reduce both the flexibility of your muscles and your **coordination**. Make sure to drink plenty of water!
· Junk food robs your body of the energy you would get from healthy food choices.

NEW WORDS

Dehydration: An unhealthy loss of water from the body.

Eat nutritious foods such as protein-rich meat, seafood, and dairy items to fuel your body for long, hard sessions. Don't forget a colorful variety of fruit and vegetables. Sleep helps your body recover from wear and tear. Get enough — about eight to ten hours per night — and watch your skate skills soar.

LOOK CLOSER

Stretching exercises

· *Ankle flex.* Sit on the floor with both legs fully extended. Lift one leg a few inches off the ground. Point your toe and use it to "write" your name in the air. Repeat with other foot.

· *Back twist.* Sit on the floor with one leg out straight and the other crossed in front of you, with the sole of your foot on the floor. Use your opposite elbow to pull the knee into your body while you twist. Repeat on the other side.

· *Groin stretch.* Sit with the bottoms of your feet touching each other. Press down gently on your knees. Hold for 20 seconds.

· *Hamstring stretch.* Lie on your back. Raise one leg. Hold it for 20 seconds. Repeat with other leg.

· *Quad stretch.* Grasp one shin. Pull it back and up toward your rear until you feel a stretch in the front of your thigh. Hold for 20 seconds. Repeat with other leg.

Stretching warms the body up and helps to prevent injuries to the muscles.

Coordination: When the body and brain work together to balance and move.

Keeping Balance

Balance is key to great skateboarding. But you'll need to be one step ahead of your brain on a skateboard — it's hard to predict where there are bumps and dips on the ground. It's even harder keeping upright when you're trying out your next trick.

Your **center of gravity** is the key to keeping balance. Its location varies based on your shape and **gender**, and it shifts whenever you move. The lower your center of gravity, the easier it is to hold your balance. Crouch low to stay stable and improve your balance.

All in the ears

Inside your ear, semicircular canals are filled with fluid. When your head moves, so does the fluid. Its motion stimulates hair cells in the walls of the canals. The cells send the information to your brain. Your brain then uses the information, along with other cues from your eyes, joints, and muscles, to figure out your position in space.

Foot stand

- Stand on one foot.
- Time yourself with a stopwatch.
- Imagine how much harder this test would be on a moving skateboard!

Crouching down low helps to lower your center of gravity.

NEW WORDS

Center of gravity: The point in your body where your weight is centered.

18

Regular or goofy?

Lefties usually find it easier to balance when they ride goofy — with their right foot forward. Righties tend to prefer a regular stance — with their left foot forward.

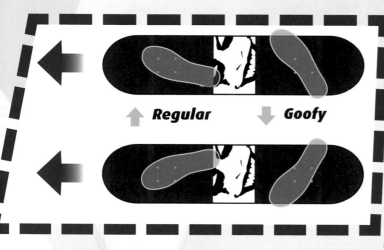

↑ **Regular**   ↓ **Goofy**

↑ **How do you ride — regular or goofy?**

Learning how to fall

When you lose your balance, protect yourself by learning how to take the fall.
1) Crouch down low so you won't have as far to fall.
2) Try to land on your shoulder and arm. Then roll to reduce the force of the impact.
3) Try not to brace your fall with your hands to avoid wrist injuries.
4) Stiffening up will cause greater damage to joints and muscles, so stay relaxed.

↓ **Your arms can help you stay balanced.**

▶▶▶▶▶▶▶▶

FACT!

Body balance
· Holding your arms like an airplane helps to maintain balance.
· Working out with a balance board can help you improve both your balance and coordination.

Gender: Whether someone is male or female.

On the Streets

A lot of street tricks seem to defy the laws of physics. In reality, skaters take advantage of physics to help them pull off the most amazing stunts.

When you pop an Ollie, you put a strong downward force on the tail. In his laws of motion, **Sir Isaac Newton** states that "for every action there is an equal and opposite reaction." So when the tail pushes down against the ground, the ground pushes up against the board with an equal and opposite force. When you jump, the upward force is able to overcome the force of **gravity**. The board pops into the air.

It takes time and practice to pop the perfect Ollie.

NEW WORDS

Sir Isaac Newton (1642-1727): English scientist who devised with the three laws of motion.

How to pop an Ollie

1) Set your stance. Stand on the board with the ball of your back foot hanging off the tail. The ball of your front foot should be in the middle of the deck, between the bolts.

2) Crouch. Keep your shoulders in line with your feet.

3) Jump. Kick down with your back foot so the board's tail hits the ground. The board should "pop" off the ground.

4) Bend your front knee and slide your front foot toward the board's nose.

5) While still in the air, bring your back knee up to your chest. Press down with your front foot. Adjust the position of both feet so that the board levels out.

6) Land both feet at the same time, one above each truck. Let your knees bend when you hit the ground to absorb the impact.

LOOK CLOSER

How did the Ollie get its name?

Alan Gelfand invented the Ollie in 1976. Gelfand's nickname was Ollie, so when he came up with the new trick, it was given the same nickname!

Gravity: The attractive force exerted by any object with mass.

Ramps and Pipes

A skater launches into the sky. Then, still in midair, he or she spins around and drops back down onto the ramp. This classic vert trick uses simple laws of physics to reach whole new heights.

To get big air, you need to be moving at top speed.

To move at high speeds, skaters crouch on the floor of the pipe and stand tall on the transition. This is called pumping. It works in the same way that pumping your legs on a swing makes you go higher and faster.

NEW WORDS

Centripetal force: The force that keeps objects moving in a circular path.

FACT!

Skate to rotate

You need to apply a twisting force to start rotating. Skaters use their arms to create the **torque** for midair turns.

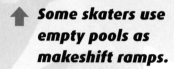

↑ *Some skaters use empty pools as makeshift ramps.*

Skating force

Centripetal force keeps objects moving along a circular path. When you skate a half-pipe, centripetal force acts on your body, keeping you in a crouch. To rise up, you need to work to overcome the force. Your extra effort produces more energy than you use, so you wind up not only beating the centripetal force, but boosting yourself up and over the lip.

LOOK CLOSER

Skating the ramp

Here's what you need to do to work the ramp:
· Drop in.
· On the floor, crouch.
· On the transition, stand up.
· Pull an Ollie at the lip and you will be airborne.
· Pull your legs up.
· Twist your upper body. Your legs and feet will turn in the opposite direction.
· Guide the board around with your front foot. Keep your legs tucked.
· As you descend, straighten your legs.
· Stay loose when you make contact. Let your knees absorb the shock.

↑ *Strength and balance are key to successful lip tricks.*

Torque: A twisting force.

Build Your Own Ramp

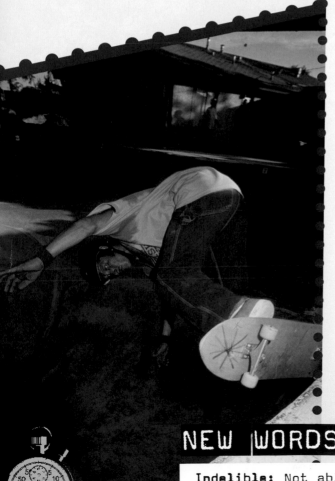

Tony Alva, one of the original Z-boys, skates in a pool.

To build your own ramp, all you need are simple materials and basic woodworking skills. Make sure an adult is available to supervise your work!

Z-boys

Back in the 70s, the Z-boys left an **indelible** mark on skateboarding. A surf shop in Venice, California, sponsored a local surfing team called the Zephyrs, or Z-boys for short. The Z-boys also skateboarded. Around that time, California was suffering from drought. A lot of people drained their swimming pools. The Z-boys would sneak into backyards and skate in the empty pools until the police showed up! Every day, the skaters would try something new. They wound up developing a new style of skateboarding. In 1975, at the *Del Mar Nationals*, the Zephyr team's thrilling moves caused a sensation. The Z-boys became stars. The team only lasted a few months before it was torn apart by fame and rivalries.

NEW WORDS

Indelible: Not able to be erased.

Build your own ramp

1) Choose plans that you like and that will fit in your available space. You can find a lot of ideas on the Internet.

2) Cut all your pieces to size.

3) Build the framework, making sure all of the bracing is sturdy.

4) Soak the top sheets of plywood in cold water for about one hour. The water will soften the wood, making it easier to curve into shape.

5) Screw the plywood top sheets onto the framework.

6) Sand and paint the ramp to reduce friction and yield a smoother ride.

Screws have threads that grip the wood and hold your joints more firmly in place than nails.

What you need

Wood for the framework
Pen
Electric or handheld saw
Wood screws
Electric drill
Duct tape
Plywood sheets
Sandpaper
Paint

Sand the lowest edge of the top sheet so it is even with the ground. Add a layer of duct tape to make the transition even smoother.

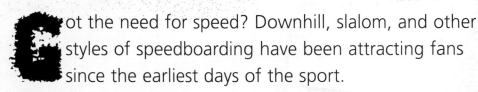

Speed and Slalom

↓ Street luge is an exciting alternative to conventional skating.

Got the need for speed? Downhill, slalom, and other styles of speedboarding have been attracting fans since the earliest days of the sport.

Downhill skaters use extra long rigid skateboards to **bomb** down hills at thrilling speeds. They wear **aerodynamic** helmets to reduce friction caused by wind resistance. Slalom skaters race through a track marked with small cones. They weave through the cones in the fastest possible time. The trick to good slalom skating is to pick the best "line" through the course. In street luge and buttboarding, riders lie on their backs and hit speeds of up to 30 mph (50 km/h).

LOOK CLOSER

Safety gear

At high speeds, safety gear is essential. Racers suit up like motorcycle riders in full leather body "armor," heavy gloves, protective footwear, and DOT helmets.

NEW WORDS

Bomb: To go downhill as fast as you can.

Gravity racing

Skateboard racing is powered only by the force of gravity — no engines are allowed. An organization called Gravity Sports International sponsors and oversees competition in all types of gravity-powered sports.

FACT!

► ► ► ► ► ► ► ►

Dead Stop!

· Slalom and downhill skaters reach speeds of 40 mph (60 km/h).
· Top racers tape their shoelaces to increase their aerodynamics.
· Sliding — a form of stopping — has developed into a new type of downhill skateboarding.

Pumping

A technique called pumping lets slalom skaters speed up with every turn they carve. To do so, skaters force their boards along an S-curved path by rocking their bodies and swinging their arms back and forth. Their motion generates so much energy that some skaters can even accelerate going up hills.

Downhill skaters accelerate down a hill during a race in Aviemore in Scotland.

LOOK CLOSER

Body position

Downhill racers crouch to decrease wind resistance and pick up speed down the hill. To slow down, they "air brake" by standing upright with arms outstretched.

Aerodynamic: Having a shape that improves the flow of air past it.

Future of Skateboarding

Michael J. Fox as Marty McFly on a hoverboard in the movie Back to the Future II (1985).

What might skateboarding look like in the future? Check out these possibilities, already in the works.

Will skateboarding, born in the laid-back world of surfing, always retain its freewheeling spirit? Maybe not. The skaters of the future will have to be ultra fit athletes to keep up with the demands of their sport. They will have to train harder and smarter. Advances in sports medicine and technology will undoubtedly be used to improve skating technique, injury recovery, and gear design.

Hoverboards

The illusion of Michael J. Fox as Marty McFly skating on a **hoverboard** looks set to become a reality. To work, these flying decks need to be super light. Look for high-tech components made of carbon nanotubes.

NEW WORDS

Hoverboard: Skateboard-type vehicle that travels on a cushion of air.

Tomorrow's skaters will train hard to cope with the physical demands of their sport.

Pro skater Danny Way launches off the DC Mega Ramp at Point X Camp, in California.

Ramping up

Imagine a half-pipe eight stories high. That's how big the megaramp is in the backyard of champion skater Bob Burnquist. As the ramps keep getting bigger, you can expect the vert tricks to get increasingly dangerous.

Skate simulation

Combine video games with the latest in **virtual reality** and what have you got? Simulated slides, flips, and turns. That's extreme skateboarding without the risk.

Virtual reality: A computer-generated world in which people can interact with their environment.

Glossary

Aerodynamic: Having a shape that improves the flow of air past it.

Axle: A rod that attaches to wheels and allows them to spin.

Bomb: To go downhill as fast as you can.

Bushing: A hollow sleeve used to reduce friction or motion in mechanical parts.

Center of gravity: The point in your body where your weight is centered.

Centripetal force: The force that keeps objects moving in a circular path.

Coordination: When the body and brain work together to balance and move.

Cruising: Using your board to move around.

Deck: The flat part of the skateboard on which the skater stands.

Dehydration: An unhealthy loss of water from the body.

Exoskeleton: An outer skeleton or shell, like an insect.

Friction: The force that opposes the movement of two surfaces that are touching one another.

Gender: Whether someone is male or female.

Gravity: The attractive force exerted by any object with mass.

Grind: To ride on a ledge or rail in such a way that only the trucks touch, making a grinding noise.

Half-cab: A ramp trick named for skater Steve Caballero.

Half-pipe: A U-shaped ramp used for skateboard tricks.

Hoverboard: Skateboard-type vehicle that travels on a cushion of air.

Immobilize: To prevent from moving.

Impact: When two objects hit each other, such as your feet and the ground.

Indelible: Not able to be erased.

Kicktail: The rise at the back of the deck.

Resilient: Being able to return to an original shape or position.

Sir Isaac Newton (1642–1727): English scientist who devised the three laws of motion.

Torque: A twisting force.

Urethane: A hard-wearing plastic that can be molded into different shapes.

Virtual reality: An computer generated world in which people can interact with their environment.

Vulcanized: Soles with sulfur added to the rubber to make the shoes harder, stronger, and more stretchy.